This book belongs to

_____

MY VERY FIRST
BOOK of

BIBLE
QUESTIONS

The Bible version used in this publication is *The New King James Version.* Copyright © 1979, 1980, 1982, Thomas Nelson, Inc.

My Very First Book of Bible Questions
ISBN 1-56292-684-5

Text copyright © 1994, 2001 by Mary Hollingsworth

Copyright © 1994, 2001 by Educational Publishing Concepts, Inc.
P.O. Box 665
Wheaton, Illinois 60189

Published by Honor Kidz
An Imprint of Honor Books, Inc.
P.O. Box 55388
Tulsa, Oklahoma 74155

MY VERY FIRST
BOOK OF

BIBLE
QUESTIONS

Mary Hollingsworth

Illustrated by
Rick Incrocci

An Imprint of Honor Books, Inc.
Tulsa, Oklahoma

Dear Parents,

Questions, questions, questions! Kids are full of questions, aren't they? On top of that, they expect *you* to have answers to all their questions.

It's amazing, when you really start thinking about it, how many of a child's questions can be answered from God's Word. As long as God is involved, things are just as they should be.

Your curious child will love this little book of Bible questions, and you will love having the answers to those questions right at your fingertips. "Who named the animals?" "Who was the oldest person who ever lived?" "Who made the world and everything in it?"

The best part about this book is that

the questions and answers will help your child learn more about God and His marvelous Word, the Bible. So let's get started!

Mary Hollingsworth

Question:
Is there more than one God?

Answer:
No

To Think About

You can help God. What can you
do to make the world better?
Just as there is only one God,
there is only one *you*! That is
because God made you to be
special.

There is one God, and there is no other but He.

Mark 12:32

Question:
Who made the world and everything in it?

Answer:
God

To Do

Look out your window and name some things you see that God made.

Look inside your house and name the people you see that God made.

In the beginning God created the
heavens and the earth.

Genesis 1:1

Question:
Who were the first people God made?

Answer:
Adam and Eve

To Think About
Where did Adam and Eve live?

To Do
Make a person out of clay.

And Adam called his wife's name
Eve, because she was the mother of
all living.

Genesis 3:20

Question:
Who named the animals?

Answer:
Adam

To Think About

What do we call the animals in
this picture?

What is your name?

Who gave you *your* name?

Adam gave names to all cattle, to the birds of the air, and to every beast of the field.

Genesis 2:20

Question:
Who was the oldest person who ever lived?

Answer:
Methuselah
(969 years old)

To Think About

How old are you?

Who is the oldest person you know?

All the days of Methuselah were nine hundred and sixty-nine years.

Genesis 5:27

Question:
Who built a great big boat to save the animals from a flood?

Answer:
Noah

To Think About

Where is Noah in this picture?

To Do

Ask an adult to put some water in the sink so you can play with a tiny boat. Think about the very big boat that Noah built.

God said to Noah . . . "Make yourself
an ark."

Genesis 6:13-14

Question:
How old was Noah when the Flood began?

Answer:
600 years old

To Do

With some paper and crayons,
draw a picture of Noah's boat in
the Flood.
Draw a rainbow in the picture to
show God's promise to never again
flood the whole world.

Noah was six hundred years old when the floodwaters were on the earth.

Genesis 7:6

Question:
Who wrestled with God and won?

Answer:
Jacob

To Do

Have a fun wrestling match with someone in your family. Be careful not to hurt each other. Ask an adult to be referee.

You have struggled with God and
with men, and have prevailed.

Genesis 32:28

Question:
Who was given a special coat with many different colors in it?

Answer:
Joseph

To Think About
What kind of coat do you wear?
Who gave you your coat? Does
that person love you?

[Israel] made [Joseph] a tunic of
many colors.

Genesis 37:3

Question:
What baby was put in a tiny boat and floated on the Nile River?

Answer:
Moses

To Do

With paper and crayons, draw a picture of baby Moses in his basket boat in the river.

Mail your picture to one of your grandparents with a note that says, "I love you."

[Moses' mother] took an ark . . . put the child in it, and laid it in the reeds by the river's bank.

Exodus 2:3

Question:
Who spoke to Moses from a burning bush that never burned up?

Answer:
God

To Do

At the burning bush, God told Moses to take his shoes off. Moses was on holy ground. If it is not too cold, take your shoes off. Walk around barefoot.

With some paper and crayons, draw a picture of a burning bush.

The bush was burning with fire, but
the bush was not [burned up].

Exodus 3:2

Question:
Who heard a donkey talk?

Answer:
Balaam

To Think About

Have you ever heard a donkey talk?

What sound does a donkey usually make instead of talking?

The Lord opened the mouth of the
donkey, and she [spoke] to Balaam.

Numbers 22:28

Question:
How many commandments did God give to Moses on Mt. Sinai?

Answer:
Ten

To Do

God's ten rules are listed in your Bible in Exodus 20:1-17. Ask an adult to help you find and read them.

Using two sheets of tablet paper, make your own pretend tablets of stone. Write God's Ten Commandments on the paper.

[God] declared . . . the Ten
Commandments; and He wrote them
on two tablets of stone.

Deuteronomy 4:13

Question:
Who helped the spies Joshua sent out escape from the enemy?

Answer:
Rahab

To Do

Pretend that you are a spy for God and that the enemy is after you! Crawl under a table or bed as if you are hiding on Rahab's roof from the soldiers.

Then [Rahab] let them down by a
rope through the window.

Joshua 2:15

Question:
What city's walls fell down?

Answer:
Jericho

To Do

Build a pretend city of Jericho out of building blocks. The city should have high walls all around it. March around the pretend Jericho seven times. Then pretend to blow a horn and carefully knock down the block walls.

The people heard the sound of the
trumpet, and the people shouted [and]
the wall fell down flat.

Joshua 6:20

Question:
Who made the sun and moon stand still?

Answer:
Joshua, with God's help

To Think About
Would you like to fly to the moon just as the astronauts did?

To Do
Say a prayer thanking God for the warm sun and pretty moon.

Then Joshua spoke to the Lord . . . so
the sun stood still, and the moon
stopped.

Joshua 10:12-13

Question:
Who was the strongest man who ever lived?

Answer:
Samson

To Think About

What are some things you can do to grow up big and strong?

To Do

Point to Samson's muscles in the picture.

And the Spirit of the Lord came
mightily upon [Samson].

Judges 14:6

Question:
Which little boy heard God call him in the night?

Answer:
Samuel

To Think About

If God talked aloud to you during the night, what would you think? When God spoke to Samuel, he said, "Here I am, Lord; I am listening." Is it important that we always listen to what God says for us to do? (Yes.)

While Samuel was lying down . . . the LORD called Samuel. And he answered, "Here I am!"

1 Samuel 3:3-4

Question:
Who was the first king of God's people?

Answer:
King Saul

To Do

The Bible says that Saul was head and shoulders taller than anyone else. Ask an adult to help you stand on a chair or table so you are taller than the adult is. How does it feel to be so tall?

All the people went to Gilgal, and there they made Saul king before the LORD.

1 Samuel 11:15

Question:
Who fought a nine-foot-tall giant and won?

Answer:
David

To Do

Ask an adult to show you how high nine feet is.
Now ask the adult to measure how tall you are.

David prevailed over the [giant] with
a sling and a stone.

1 Samuel 17:50

Question:
What was the name of David's special friend?

Answer:
Jonathan

To Think About

What is your best friend's name?
What do you like to do with your
best friend?

Jonathan loved [David] as his own soul.

1 Samuel 18:1

Question:
What kind of birds brought food to Elijah the prophet?

Answer:
Ravens

To Think About

Who told the ravens to take food to Elijah? Will God take care of you, too?

To Do

Use crayons and paper, to draw a picture of a raven.

The ravens brought [Elijah] bread and meat in the morning, and bread and meat in the evening.

1 Kings 17:6

Question:
What man did not die but went up to heaven in a whirlwind?

Answer:
Elijah the prophet

To Do

With some paper and crayons, draw a picture of a whirlwind. Pretend that you are a whirlwind and carefully spin around and around in circles.

Elijah went up by a whirlwind into heaven.

2 Kings 2:11

Question:
Who was the wisest man who ever lived?

Answer:
Solomon

To Think About

What can you do to be wise like Solomon was?

Who is the wisest person you know?

God said to Solomon, " . . . Wisdom
and knowledge are granted to you."
2 Chronicles 1:11-12

Question:
What queen saved all her people from being killed?

Answer:
Queen Esther

To Do

Ask an adult to help you make a crown out of construction paper. Wear the crown and pretend you are Queen Esther helping her people.

Who knows whether you [Esther]
have come to the kingdom for such a
time as this?

Esther 4:14

Question:
Who saw dry bones come back to life?

Answer:
Ezekiel the prophet

To Do

Pretend that you are a pile of bones on the floor. Now, slowly get up as if you are coming back to life.

Now that you are alive again, do a little dance to show just how lively you are!

There was a noise, and suddenly a
rattling; and the bones came together,
bone to bone.

Ezekiel 37:7

Question:
Who spent the night in a deep pit with wild lions but did not get hurt?

Answer:
Daniel

To Think About

Who saved Daniel from being eaten by the lions? (God.)

To Do

Using a brown paper bag, make a mask of a lion with a smile on its face.

[God] has delivered Daniel from the power of the lions.

Daniel 6:27

Question:
Who was swallowed by a giant fish but lived to tell about it?

Answer:
Jonah

To Think About

How do you think it would feel to be inside a giant fish?

To Do

Ask an adult to take you to the zoo or a pet store to see fish in a big aquarium.

Jonah was in the belly of the fish
three days and three nights…. And it
[spit] Jonah onto dry land.

Jonah 1:17; 2:10

Question:
Who came to earth to save all people?

Answer:
Jesus Christ

To Think About

Are the children in this picture happy that Jesus came to save them?

Are you happy that Jesus came to save you, too?

[Jesus] has power on earth to forgive sins.

Matthew 9:6

Question:
Who is Jesus?

Answer:
The Son of God

To Think About

If Jesus were here right now, what would you tell Him?

To Do

Say a prayer to God thanking Him for Jesus.

[Jesus] who is to be born will be
called the Son of God.

Luke 1:35

Question:
Who was the mother of Jesus?

Answer:
Mary

To Do

Find a doll, or use a pillow, and wrap it in a blanket like the baby Jesus.

Sing a lullaby to the baby.

They saw [Jesus] with Mary His mother.

Matthew 2:11

Question:
Who told some shepherds that Jesus the Savior had been born?

Answer:
Angels

To Think About

If you heard angels singing, what do you think their voices would sound like?

If you saw angels, what do you think they would look like?

The angel said to [the shepherds],
" . . . There is born to you this day a
Savior, who is Christ the Lord."

Luke 2:10-11

Question:
Where was baby Jesus born?

Answer:
In Bethlehem

To Think About

What animal sounds do you think baby Jesus heard while He was lying in the manger?

To Do

Try to make some of the sounds He heard.

The shepherds said to one another,
"Let us now go to Bethlehem. . . ."
And they . . . found . . . [Jesus]
lying in a manger.

Luke 2:15-16

Question:
Who brought special gifts to Jesus?

Answer:
Wise men from the East

To Think About

What kind of animals did the wise men ride as they came to find Jesus?

Would you like to ride a camel someday? What would be fun about riding a camel?

[The wise men] presented gifts to Him: gold, frankincense, and myrrh [perfume].

Matthew 2:11

Question:
What did the wise men follow to find the baby Jesus?

Answer:
A bright star

To Do

Make a big yellow star out of construction paper. Hang it in your room to remind you of Jesus.
Ask an adult to go outside with you at night. Look for a bright star like the one the wise men saw.

The star . . . went before them, till it came and stood over where the young Child was.

Matthew 2:9

Question:
How many apostles did Jesus choose to help Him?

Answer:
Twelve

To Do

Count from one to twelve.
The names of Jesus' twelve
apostles are listed in your Bible in
Luke 6:13-16. Ask an adult to help
you find and read their names.

[Jesus] called His disciples to
Himself; and from them He chose
twelve . . . apostles.

Luke 6:13

Question:
Which apostle walked to Jesus on the water?

Answer:
Peter

To Think About

Are people supposed to be able to walk on the water?

Who helped Peter walk on the water? (Jesus.)

When Peter had come down out of the boat, he walked on the water to go to Jesus.

Matthew 14:29

Question:
Who was so short that he had to climb up in a tree to see Jesus?

Answer:
Zacchaeus

To Do

Have someone measure you to see how tall you are.

To Think About

Think about how you feel when you are in a crowd where everyone is taller than you.

[Zaccheus] sought to see who Jesus was, but could not because . . . he was . . . short.

Luke 19:3

Question:
Who is known as the father of the Jewish people?

Answer:
Abraham

To Think About

How many people are in your family?

To Do

Point to all of Abraham's children in picture.

Abraham, who is the father of us all.

Romans 4:16

Question:
Who inspired the Bible?

Answer:
God

To Do

On a piece of paper write the
letters *B-I-B-L-E*.
When you say your prayers
tonight, thank God for the Bible,
His wonderful Word.

[The Bible] is given by inspiration of God.

2 Timothy 3:16

Additional copies of this book
and other books in this series are available
from your local bookstore.

My Very First Book of Bible Fun Facts
My Very First Book on God
My Very First Book of Bible Lessons
My Very First Book of Prayers
My Very First Book of Bible Heroes
My Very First Book of Bible Words
My Very First Book of God's Animals

If you have enjoyed this book, or if it has
impacted your life, we would like to hear from you.
Please contact us at:

Honor Kidz
Department E
P.O. Box 55388
Tulsa, Oklahoma 74155
Or by e-mail at info@honorbooks.com